SPEAK

Sarah Clarke

CONTENTS

THANK YOU

I just want to take a few moments to thank the people that have really sown into me whether we have walked side by side or you have supported me threw pray or financially. I just want you to know how utterly grateful I am to have you in my life and what a privilege it has been to journey with you.

I want to thank all my family especially my dad and my sister for really sticking with me when at times it's been extremely difficult, without even realising it you have been my biggest help when I have wanted to throw in the towel. I want to thank my Nanna Pauline because she is an absolute gem and has supported me all the way threw and has one of the biggest hearts I know. A massive shout out to my beautiful daughter Melody Rose who is such an incredible treasure
#WhenWeHaveEachotherWeHaveEverything

I want to thank Bridge Street Community Church for your support financially over the years and practically as well as pray fully, Pastor Andy Lenton is a good man with a very kind heart. My friends that I've made over the years, and those on the outreach that never stop I just want to say a big thank you.
#FaithCanMoveMountains

Thank you to Horizon Life Training for being so amazing and supportive in all that we do together as a team. To my manager you are a beautiful women and thank you for your hard work, leadership and gracious heart.
#HisMerciesAreNewEveryMorning

I want to thank everyone at Sherwood Church who have earnestly prayed for me. Pastor Phil and Lynn Hills who helped me, pushed me and was generously gracious towards me and taught me that giving up was never an option (You are amazing people). Thank you for being there you became my spiritual mum Lynn, you loved me and showed me that I was so much more than what I believed I was.
#TheGenerousWillProsper

I want to thank everyone at Revive Church. Thank you so much for your hearts and generosity, you really helped me in many ways. You gave me a chance and welcomed me into your family and for that I am truly grateful.
#TheJoyOfTheLordIsYourStrength

Huge thanks to Alison Fenning for encouraging me with this book and mentoring me it's very much appreciated
#TrulyMySoulFindsRestInGod

I just want to thank my heavenly Father for keeping me through every hurdle I have faced in my life, threw the ups and the downs. You have truly been my rock and my best friend, the lover of my soul and my saviour. I never in a million years thought this moment could or would ever exist with me writing a book inspired by your spirit. Thank you for everything because I am so grateful and my heart is just overwhelmed by your love, your grace and your kindness.

I have known you to be good and faithful to your word and you have never let me down but choose every day to pursue me. Such beauty, I am just in love with you and thank you for your goodness and restoration in my life. **#PraiseForHeaviness**

MY STORY...

Firstly, I just want to start off by saying you have a testimony and your testimony matter's, I love this quote "what God is bringing you through is going to be the testimony that will bring somebody else through, he turn's your mess into his glorious message"

Testimonies can be used to empower, to build up and to be an example of the power of God in our lives and to give him the glory, we are overcomers because he first overcame.

Revelations 12:11 Amplified Bible (AMP)
"And they overcame and conquered him because of the blood of the Lamb and because of the word of their testimony"

So today I want to share with you how I overcame areas of addiction in my life and how the strongholds of my broken inner self were broken down and slowly built back up. This is a beautiful picture of the Father's restoration and mercy in my life.

To know his love is to be at one with him.

Isaiah 61:7 New International Version (NIV)
"Instead of your shame you will receive a double portion, and instead of disgrace you will rejoice in your inheritance. And so you will inherit a double portion in your land and everlasting Joy will be yours"
Amen.

Paint the picture

It was a dark night; it was really quiet. I remember feeling dead on the inside as I laid in bed hoping I wouldn't wake up, curtains shut. Closed off from the world around me to scared to step outside as the voices in my head ran wild, thinking people were trying to kill me as I jumped at the wind blowing the tree branches' against the window. My heart pounding as I sat in total fear thinking "my only way out was to die" the voices got louder, they told me to give up and that I needed to finish myself off. One voice spoke so loud and told me that nobody would come for me and that I had been forgotten, alone left to fester in this mess that I had got myself in.

In a steric I crawled onto my knees and started to let out this huge cry, it came from somewhere deep, from the pit of my stomach. **"God if you are real, if you can hear me then please kill me I want to die. I can't do this anymore, please help me"** in a mess I got into bed and cried myself to sleep, little did I know that my life was about to change in a way I had never imagined.

I awoke in a prison, it was dark! I was scared and needed to escape. I don't know how but I managed to get out. I ran as fast as I could but someone had started to chase me I turned around and to my absolute horror, it was me? I was chasing myself? Frantic I ran faster and faster. She tried to grab me as I came to a cliff hanger, within seconds I decided to jump off the cliff hanger into the deep water's. I swam, I swam and right in front of me appeared this huge ship and waiting for me was Jesus. He took a hold of me and helped me onto the boat but I never saw his face.

I felt like I was in the safest place. He sat me down and took a hold of my hand it was fire, like glory; something I have never seen before, something so beautiful. In that moment I was filled with his love, his presence and Jesus said these words' to me **"Sarah I love you"** he called me by name, I was his **"keep persevering"** such encouragement made me feel like I wasn't forgotten I had been predestined and my life had purpose.

This moment, this encounter of Jesus Christ changed my heart but my mind was still poorly. I knew I had been touched by the real living God and that this wasn't a hype it was real and I wasn't losing my mind but for the first time had such a sense of belonging and freedom. What now? Shortly after with some much needed help from different people God brought into my life I went into a Christian rehab called Betel.

I remember before going into this rehab Jesus uttering this in my heart **"pick up your cross and follow me"**. I knew that this was it all them prays of desperation, all them secret letters to God. He saw each one and finally answered my pray of getting out and leaving this life behind, I thought in this instant that I was ready and felt that this was my time.

Unfortunately, this didn't last and so I left this rehab just 4 months later but not before finding a book called **"as white as snow"** written by a woman who had completed the Teen Challenge programme in Wales. I read the book and couldn't believe it, this woman had my life and she was abused. Nobody wanted her but she met with Jesus who had called me by name, this same Jesus.

My heart was set ablaze, I urgently got down on my knees once again and cried out to God to send me to this Hope House, where they do chapel, teachings and have counselling. I knew that this place called Teen Challenge was a special place and that I needed to go there because something was their waiting for me and I didn't know what it was.

Then this happened, straight away after leaving Betel I was back to where I started apart from this time I was homeless. My family wouldn't take me in but who could blame them id destroyed the trust and relationship I had with them, even my dad was disappointed and he is always there trying to help me.

My best friend at the time took me in and I thought yes it's going to be amazing, I remember opening a can of larger and in my gut I felt Holy Spirit say to me **"what are you doing this isn't you, don't do this"** I felt instantly convicted but I continued. When we came to the cocaine at first I was hesitant but that on the inside of me took over as I began to sniff a line I felt a buzz, I felt alive and in control and nobody was stopping me now. What made it worst was my former best friends ex-boyfriend had said this to me **"welcome back to hell"** for the first time I felt the fear of God and began to tremble on the inside.

My close friend from church who supported me all the way through rehab rung me up the next day, he was such an amazing encouragement for me and didn't ever judge me at all which was strange to me at the time. He asked where I was and how I was doing as he heard I left Betel rehab centre and I was honest, I had relapsed back into a deep pit of self-destruction and needed help. Next to my friend at the time was a woman who had worked for Teen Challenge in the past, we chatted about me going to this Hope House that a few weeks ago I had been praying about. She had asked me outright if I wanted it and I said yes, desperate and in need to get out of the entanglement that I was in I said I'd do anything.

Suddenly things started to make sense, a couple came up to me and offered me to stay with them until I went into this Teen Challenge. They had told me that God had told them that they needed to take me in, people were buying me clothes and items I needed. I met up with an amazing woman who worked on the Teen Challenge Leeds outreach team.

She just reflected everything of Jesus that I'd never seen in a woman before, she just loved people and kept telling me my eyes were so beautiful and how Jesus had an amazing plan over my life. She saw something good in me and encouraged me, she saw straight into my heart even at its most broken, with her I felt safe and warm. She worked with me for around 5 weeks as we filled out an application form for Teen Challenge, she encouraged me in the waiting of this even when things got dark.

It was around bonfire night of November 2015 and my church friends had gathered together to have a social event and watch the fireworks but little did they know I was drunk and had secretly stashed alcohol in my coat. Plan was to sneak off after 30mins to catch up with other friends but they managed to talk to into going around to their house for some good food and treats.

This didn't go down well and I ended up being locked into one of their flats coming face to face with my demons and realising I had a serious problem with alcohol. They were all good friends to me and to this day I thank each one for helping me through that time in my life, in that moment something significant took place as I poured my last can of larger down the sink.

I had a real taste of freedom…

Some weeks later we drove up to Wales leaving the past behind

Isaiah 43:19 New International Version (NIV)
"See, I am doing a new thing! Now it springs up; do you not perceive it? I am making a way in the wilderness and streams in the wasteland."

I was asleep for the majority of the trip, when we arrived I think I was overwhelmed with so much emotion I just didn't know what to do. Walking into Teen Challenge Hope House was beautiful, the staff were really nice and welcoming with me even though I wanted to scream on the inside. I guess It was different because I had never felt love like this before and at time's I felt I had to pinch myself.

I remember having an adviser once a week to talk things threw and I remember looking right into her eyes and saying **"Is there any hope for me?"** I just felt so hopeless and scared and felt like I was damaged goods. I believed every lie I heard in my mind and thought **"What could God do with my life?"**

But something inside of my soul would not give up the fight for my freedom.

Romans 12:2 Amplified Bible (AMP)
"And do not be conformed to this world (any longer with its superficial values and customs), but be transformed and progressively changed (as you mature spiritually) by the renewing of your mind (focusing on godly values and ethical attitudes), so that you may prove (for yourselves) what the will of God is, that which is good and acceptable and perfect (in His plan and purpose for you)."

Completing the Teen Challenge programme was one of the hardest things I have ever had to do but Jesus brought me threw it. I'll be honest because many times I felt like I was going to die because of the inward pain I carried, I really had to fight my way through various obstacles and deep rooted issues like rejection, rage and self-hatred. I use to hide in the chapel with my head in my bible or on the keyboard singing, praying and speaking in tongues just to be close to Jesus. My main pray was **"Lord please stop the voice's"**. In 2011 I was diagnosed with a borderline personality disorder amongst other things and at one point told I had borderline schizophrenia. I use to think about suicide a lot when I was in Teen Challenge but never really told anyone the depth of what I felt because I was so scared they would send me away to a hospital if they knew how poorly I was and that was my worst nightmare. I thought if I seek God then everything else would be added and my mind would be healed.

My heart slowly began to change as I persisted with what I was being taught and I started to receive the love of God which washed over me. I had encountered God's word and it slowly started to renew my mind, I started to see things clearer as things became new to me. Many of time's I was touched by Gods power but his word anchored and sustained me, it was his word that came alive as I started to see the fruit of applying it to my life. I could finally turn the light off at night because I found peace and began to believe what I was praying out. After living a life in a prison in my mind I could feel myself becoming really free. At one point I thought this was impossible because I thought I was too far gone that there was no hope for me but in God's word he says in Matthew 19:26 Amplified Bible (AMP)

"But Jesus looked at them and said, "With people [as far as it depends on them] it is impossible, but with God all things are possible."

This is his promise to his children and I started to believe this for my own life, that in God there are all these possibilities. I remember praying **"Lord help my unbelief"**, I remember thinking how could God choose or even love someone like me. But I had to learn how to renew my mind by his truth's and tear down the lies that I had believed over myself and over my life and that was one of the biggest giant's I have ever had to stand and face but praise God for breakthrough.

I eventually graduated the Teen Challenge programme in September 2017 which was an incredible celebration, I was able to live my dream out and sing in the worship band on stage in which my family came to see. I believe it was a miracle orchestrated by God for me to finish and complete the programme but what a sigh of relief as they called out my name on stage. I stood there in awe, Teen Challenge had thrown me a life jacket and I had finally swam to shore safe and sound.

What next?

After completing the Teen Challenge programme, I applied to study at the Teen Challenge Leadership Academy training up in leadership and outreach which was a fantastic experience. This enabled me to help and reach out to men and women in addiction giving them hope through mine and other people's stories that have come through the programme like me. I grew a lot here and was challenged in many ways, if I am really honest I have come through some tough battles during this time of my life. I made some mistakes and lived threw them by leaning on God and his word, at one point I lost friends to addiction and other's died. My faith was shaken and tested as I had so many questions and I was deeply grieving, I struggled to fully surrender.

I remember been emotionally burnt out because I came towards the end of my time at the leadership academy and I simply had nowhere to go or live. My pastor and chief executive of Teen Challenge was very gracious and kind towards me giving his time and encouragement. At this time, I had a short break away in Wales to get some rest and figure things out in my life. What was I going to do? Where was I going to go? Has God really got a plan for me? Let's be real, it was awful at times.

God really allowed me to go through these things here to heal me and set me free of some mind sets and issues I still had. I felt really close to him like he was in the room with me at times. He spoke to me so clear about bible college and about being more grounded in theology. I didn't think twice I told my pastor and began my journey to bible college.

I starting volunteering at the Teen Challenge charity shop which I absolutely loved because Lynn who is the chief executive's wife was amazing. She was just so real and down to earth which helped me to become comfortable around her.

We became close and she mentored me which I really needed. Lynn helped me with getting my finances in order, taught me about principles and just how to live an honest life in the community as a Christian woman. I went to their church called Sherwood Church and just served where I could whether it was on projector, doing teas and coffees or welcoming people because I just loved being a part of there family.

This taught me how to serve and remain faithful in the waiting which reminds me of Joseph and his attitude towards his brother's. Joseph served in humility and kept his heart right no matter what the cost and in return God blessed his with position, restoration and favour.

Genesis 50:20 (NLT)
You intended to harm me, but God intended it all for good. He brought me to this position so I could save the lives of many people.

I also volunteered at a women's organization coming alongside women with mental health doing crafts which was fun as I wanted to give back and encourage women to be the best that they can be. I didn't realize how God was working in the background of all this and giving me the tools I needed for the future. I graduated the Teen Challenge Leadership Academy in Sept 2018 full of hope and excitement for my life.

I moved out of Teen Challenge and hit a slight bump in the road with moving into the wrong place so I came back and tried again. Again God connected me to the YMCA hostel's as a friend who worked there helped me and got me a room. I will be honest; it was different to my life inside of Teen Challenge. I was no longer in a bubble of cotton wool but had been introduced to reality and that hit me like a ton of bricks crashing down onto the ground.

This hostel gave me a roof over my head and they were very generous with support but it just didn't work for me as I felt like I was going backwards. Lynn came alongside me and encouraged me. I had to put into practice all that I had learnt and had to trust God and believe that I could do it and it would only take time and perseverance. Lynn was right and with that I started to live a normal life out in the community.

I remember this scripture been real key to me during this point and that I would read it all the time and start to declare it over myself knowing that the Lord had a hold of my hand and he wasn't letting me go

Isaiah 41:13
"For I am the Lord your God who takes a hold of your right hand and say's to you, do not fear; I will help you"

I battled with temptations and ill health so I began to pray every day on my knees believing that God had a plan for my life. I believed that no matter what circumstances I faced there was a plan and purpose to this and that no matter what I couldn't run away. God really provided for me financially and built more restoration up with my family as I continued to press in.

I was going to a soup kitchen where I built up some great friendships and was able to help others in ministering through music as I love to sing and worship. When I had church or bible study I would just sit there and soak up every word that was spoken and then after I'd go home and go over each word and meditate on what God was saying and try to walk it out daily.

I started to fast and pray and bible college came back up so I continued to pursue this and have conversations with my pastor and went to visit regent's bible college which looked incredible. **A friend of mine at this time gave me this scripture as I had a vision on my heart she didn't know about but God was preparing me for what was to come**

Habakkuk 2:3
"For the vision is yet for the appointed (future) time, it hurries toward the goal (of fulfilment); it will not fail. Even though it delays, wait (patiently) for it, because it will certainly come; it will not delay."

One night one of my other friends tagged me in a post on Facebook college Revive Church College so I had a really good look at their page and their website, read testimonies and looked at what they did. Something on the inside on me leaped for joy as I started to read **TRAINING UP THE NEXT GENERATION OF REVIVALIST** my heart started to beat as I thought this is it. I remember praying and seeking counsel, God gave me a picture of Revive Church College burning with fire and Regents Bible College was in black and white.

This was a turning point for me because my heart was burning for revival and I knew from the inside out that this was the place I needed to be. With that said I messaged the tutor and straight away I met his wife at a women's conference called Cherish, ha! God has a sense of humour doesn't he, I mean right in the middle of a conference we had a chat. After this I went to visit Revive Church on a taster weekend and absolutely fell in love with it! I loved the people there and knew that they carried something different that I'd seen before in my pastor and his wife, there was a wrestle at first because the course wasn't accredited but I believed God has called me.

Moving on

I decided to go for it and say yes and I am not joking the moment I did it was like something broke and the peace of God came flooding into my room, it was amazing as started to utter **"You are good, so good; Ohh your never gonna let, never gonna let me down"** I got louder and louder just getting lost in his presence.

Thanking him for his faithfulness and goodness in my life for not leaving me or forsaking me but for standing with me always. This was such a breaking point for me as I saw the Lord's favour at work in my life, not only his favour but wow he was good and he was faithful and still is!

Lamentations 3:22-24 (AMP)
"It is because of the Lord's loving kindnesses that we are not consumed, because his (tender) compassions never fail. They are new every morning; Great and beyond measure is your faithfulness."

Shortly after making my decision about going to Revive Church College the tutor had helped me with funding for my living arrangements. I then received £500 to do the actual course from two very good friends of mine and they bought me a study bible, when I was leaving church Lynn and Phil had bought me a beautiful pink NIV bible that I could use daily as mine was a wreck. I received £100 pound in vouchers to buy college items with like my folders, books and pens and a pastor from a different church gave me his laptop which I was so grateful for (**Talk about favour**).

I moved again but this time I moved to Hull and became an intern at Revive Church College which was absolutely AWESOME, like wow what wonderful and encouraging people to be around. I first started the term with two American ladies we had some great and challenging times together in and out of ministry.

I was on my own journey during this point, previously I had ruined my hair again because me dying it and of my living arrangements prior to moving to Hull my hair had started to clump and fall out due to stress so I started to wear wigs. I didn't realise I was hiding my authentic self and God all through that first term was giving me a deeper understanding of who I was in him. I did know my worth but knowing your worth in God wow what a life changing revelation I had. Because of this revelation in January 2019 I decided to take my wig off and I felt something significant happen, I felt like I began to step into the person I was meant to be the person God has created me to be.

1 Corinthians 5:17

"Therefore, if anyone is in Christ, the new creation has come: the old has gone, the new is here!"

I sat under the teaching of my tutor and Revive Church and listened and became teachable in my ways of learning and I would ask constant questions. My tutor was so patient with me, I use to watch him all the time because he walked in a real Godly authority, he was really gifted and anointed along with his wife that's so creative. It made me want to study more and God started to speak to me in a deeper way than I'd ever had before.

I started to hear from God myself a lot clearer as I spent time in worship and pray, I started having an intimate relationship with the holy spirit and began to know him as friend and God as father which I had never had before. I remember praying for people and things would start to happen and God's power would break out, it was amazing.

I got to take part in a written interview in Christian premiere magazine and in a newspaper speaking about the goodness of our God, I was able to go into UCB radio and speak about my story to help people and point them to Jesus. Door's started to open as I was being asked to speak at events, churches and got the chance to speak at a prison in which I met some amazing people.
The church was a really family church which taught me a lot about my own family and brought healing to my heart and relationships which I needed. I began to have a restoration with my sister and we grew extremely close which was beautiful as she could see a change in my life. I

continued ongoing contact with my daughter and started to share my new life more openly with my family in which they came to visit on different occasions.

I was privileged to be able to go on mission at different churches all around the UK – I hadn't been on a plane since I was about 12 and here I was going to Ireland on a ministry trip sharing my testimony and what God can do with a life that just says yes.

I then was able to be a part of some worship in the kids and youth ministry which was awesome as I came alongside an awesome team. A couple who runs the kids and youth ministry really looked out for me, they were kind and generous towards me and I have a real gratitude for them. I met 2 women who work closely with the church helping men and women break free out of debt. They gave me time and shared their home to me and I have fond memories of our time together and still keep in touch to this day.

There were so many people that I haven't mentioned who I journeyed with at different points in Revive Church, they pulled out the gifting's in me and really released me and stirred me on to be all that God has created me to be and because of them I have grown so much more.

Thank you

1 Thessalonians 5:11 (ESV)
"Therefore, encourage one another and build one another up, just as you are doing."

Albania

I remember going to Albania for an 8 week stay in Tirana at the **Fire School of Pray** where I learnt about strategic pray and my own gifts and abilities. I was gently pushed and released to pray for Albania as a nation and helped to lead them in pray meetings. I battled with stepping up as I wouldn't have called myself a leader but I knew God had called me to lead these people to pray for their country. I remember coming alongside an incredible woman of God from America, she was so wise and encouraged me to step out in boldness, there was also a worshipper who prayed with us.

I remember a great couple from Revive church that I became good friends with who have and continue to input goodness into my life. They had kept in touch with me during my time away and helped me grow so much in pray and intercession. I remember them asking me questions and checking in with me and praying for me when it was a struggle as I was away from my family and especially my daughter. This was the time where I truly learnt how to turn warship in worship, I just let go and let out a sound out from my lips and realised; **I had a voice and a unique sound that God wanted to hear and use. This place became my training ground for 8 weeks, I felt released to sing over Albania and to declare the word of God over the nations that God had put on my heart.**

We as a team would fast and pray for 2-3 hours before the actual pray meeting and God would move intensely across the room and bring prophetic words and healing over people. I met roman gypsies who believed in God and I saw their poverty but they were so happy at heart and it just made me smile. They had nothing, yet they seemed to have everything which was humbling and beautiful at the same time.

This made me become more grateful for what I had and more thankful for my life and of the little things around that we as humanely take for granted. There was a moment that really changed my heart – there was a woman and her husband that came to lead the school for one week bringing worship and tying it in with pray.

We were all stood worshipping together really going for it and the Lord had said this to me **"lay down"** so I did just that and then I found myself in a foetal position on the floor. He then told me to **close my eyes** (as I had opened them whilst laid on the floor) so I did and what happened next I will never forget, I saw Jesus (not his face) he put his hand on my head and held the side of my face then he put my hand on his heart and said this **"Listen to the rhythm of my heart". I never fully understood what that meant until now, you see the father wants us to listen to his heart and when we do we hear what he wants to say without any of our own motives. Since this moment the lord has spoken to me so clear at times it has almost been like he was in the room with me, this never scared me but only caused me to love and pursue him more so.**

Jeremiah 33:3 (ESV)
"Call to me and I will answer you, and will tell you great and hidden things that you have not known."

Albania was a life changing time for me and I will never forget the amazing people I met or how God met with me. Coming back was just different, I had changed and something in me was different.

The end of the road

Coming to the end of my time at Revive Church College I had no idea what I was going to do. My tutor really started to like me ha ha, jokes aside he saw great potential in me and wanted to see me fulfil the calling over my life. He offered me a full time Internship and was looking into part time bible college for me to study theology and look towards gaining a degree. As much as I wanted to stay here (seriously!!!) I just couldn't find anywhere to live that was suitable for me.

Prior to this I saw an ad online that a job post had come up at Horizon Life Training Centre which was the new 'Women's Move On' centre for Christian rehabilitation. Here I would be an intern duty officer training up as a support worker coming alongside women. I would help them to become independent and up-skilled in education and to gain freedom and stability back into the community. Wow this was an amazing opportunity for me and it was what I'd always wanted to do, so spoke to my pastor and he really encouraged me and was kind me to as he just smiled.

In that moment I remembered a conversation 3 years ago that I had with a Teen Challenge Outreach Worker in Leeds. I stood there with her in a mess, hopeless coming from a life of addiction and mental health, she said this **"When you finish the Teen Challenge Rehabilitation Programme Sarah you will work at the Black Bull hotel (Horizon Life Training Women's Centre)".** I was filled with hope and confidence as I filled out the application form that maybe this God really did want me to help other women like me.

After speaking to my pastor I just went for it and filled out an application, worried as my handwriting was terrible. I hadn't filled out a job application in years Id told myself but I prayed with hope and great expectation that I was chosen to do this and that God had called me. Was this always apart of God's plan and could I really do this? the answer was yes; I was chosen to do this before the foundation of the earth, I just had to believe and take ahold of the promise of God over my life.

Brand new thing

I made a decision to leave Hull and to enter into this new promise land that God had laid before my eyes, I remember crying on the phone to my friend thinking "what am I doing" as I didn't want to lose this new family that I was a part of but needed to follow where God was leading which was hard. I moved back to my sisters and was living on her sofa for a couple of month's which wasn't ideal but I just stepped out in faith and did what I thought the Lord was telling me to do. I remember having a phone call which led to me coming back as a guest to stay at the Teen Challenge Leadership Academy until my new job/intern at Horizon Life Training had opened.

Unfortunately, it wasn't ready so I was waiting in anticipation praying constantly and hearing from the manager who was just so kind and supportive, they came together as a team (Horizon Life Training) and began to pray. I started to volunteer back at the Teen Challenge Charity shop in which God reminded me to continue to serve where I was at and to be faithful in the little that God was giving me. A short time after visiting family I decided to stay with my sister to be close to my daughter because building my relationship with her was important to me.

During this time God started to speak to me about getting ready for this season in my life and how I was to watch him move in a new way and that I was only going to go forward forgetting what once was.

Isaiah 43:18
"Forget the former things; do not dwell on the past.
See! I am doing a new thing, now it springs up; do you not
perceive it? I am making a way in the wilderness and
streams in the wasteland."

And here I am right now sat here in the office where I'm now an Intern Duty Officer in training to be a support worker helping women and propelling them into all that God has created them to be. My story still continues with even greater restoration with my daughter, beautiful

friendships that I am slowly building up and a lifetime of overflowing joy and grace I've picked up along the way.
Still completely free from drugs and alcohol 5 years later, medication free and in my right mind.

To be here is a miracle but this is our God; he turns the impossibilities into possibilities, he turns pain into promise and he turns our mess into he's glorious message.

"We step into surrender; we step out into freedom."

-Amen

And be not conformed to this *world* but be *transformed* by the *renewing* of your *mind*

Introduction

Speak, for me is a journey of the inward wrestle we all have at times in our Christian walk whether that's in the mind or heart. I really feel that I wanted to share the mind's eye of what actually goes on in our hearts whilst walking with the father, we see that running through its theme it always comes back to praise or even recognising who he is as appose to allowing the circumstances of life wash over us.

Speak is such a poetic sense of depth and truths that go on all around us and I wanted to just capture this and share with you that you're not alone, you are never alone as Father God is with us amid the pain. His love is deeper and his desire to want to be with us outweighs those bad days, just having that inward knowing of having a heavenly father. This just blows my mind away every time I think about how much he loves us, loves me; love this verse song of songs 2:4 "He brought me to the banqueting house and his banner over me is love".

You see, when I wrote each one of these spoken words of poetry it was from a place of encounter, it was from a place of intimacy with the Father. Each time he would speak to me I had an overwhelming sense of his presence upon me whether I was in the bathroom, doing the washing, on the bus and even as I was cleaning the house etc, I just felt so close. When I went over to an intense fire school of pray in

Albania to study pray, I had an encounter with Jesus that really changed my perspective and opened my heart up to not only listen but to give myself to him in relationship wholeheartedly.

To truly understand in my heart, I needed to take two steps back to allow Jesus the room he needed so he could speak, this really changed me and brought me to a place where I was able to just dwell in his presence and be with him with no motives. This one experience happened unexpectedly, I was really going for it in worship like you do you know giving it my all when I felt a quiet nudge to just lay down, so I did and in that moment I found myself in like a fetal position utterly lost in the Lord's presence.

From the moment I closed my eyes I saw the eyes of Jesus starring straight back at me just gazing at me with such love such beauty, he started to just gently embrace me by touching my head and then he took a hold of my hand and placed it onto his heart and said these words "Tune in and Listen to the rhythm of my heart beat". Since this moment something inside of me clicked and even connected more that I hadn't experienced before, I felt for me I was going into a deeper place and I had to be opened internally.

My pray for each of my reader's is this. I pray that each blockage would be removed as you read each spoken word, that Father God would take a hold of your heart and begin a deep work unplugging, un-filtering what you have picked up along the way of your own personal journey. That each insecurity that is taking you captive would be released right now in Jesus mighty name and that you would begin to stand in your given identity as a Son or daughter of the most high God. I pray that you will not be the same after reading this, but something will go and that burden that has been holding you down would be lifting off right now in Jesus name. You have belonging, you are strong with his great strength, you are victorious, and you have a purpose and a plan over your life which will come into completion in Jesus name. Lord I pray that you would pour out your grace on my sister and my brother, how we need your grace in our lives.

Thank you Father for your goodness and kindness that you shower upon us daily, we give you all the honour and glory

Amen...

walking
with my
Father

Walking with my Father

Ohh daddy I see your face, its shinning threw this broken place with colours that reflect so brightly and bold. I see your heart and you say to me

"My children come to me and take a hold, just look at my creation and tell me of the beauty that you see". I reply with "Ohh daddy! I can't believe you have chosen me.

The hills come alive with only one word from your lips and the animals walk, look daddy they crawl and even sit.

You have the authority to speak to the mountains, seas and even to the stars in the sky! Ohh look daddy even the birds can fly.

Wow look at what YOU have created so amazing and so great and your always on time, you're never late.

Day by day you create something new, Daddy speaks "I love you my daughter"

I reply with "Ohh Daddy... I love you to!" Daddy speaks "Come now daughter, let's go and explore!

" I reply with "you deserve the glory daddy, even deserve so much more.

I See You

I guess believing without seeing is persevering. Thinking and wandering on what's to come, some say creates hope? What do you do when you emotionally can't cope?

FEELING STUCK!

And not moving and that's when you begin to drown. In that moment when you become lost, that's when you're found. Even as a Christian we can all become numb and lose motivation of heart. We come to a place of yelling

BUT GOD I CAN'T!!!

The pain of the struggle becomes so intense that you naturally start to live for pretence. The words "I'm fine" just flow off your tongue and that's when you realise you're on the run. The pain of the wrestle becomes too much- the memories, the smell and even the touch. You cry out more and more, you plead with God

OPEN A NEW DOOR.

I just want to tell you that just because nothing happens straight away doesn't mean he's not listening because he's only a breath away. He doesn't give up on you because you stuff up, he's your father and loves you and wants to clean you up!

When you feel like you can't go on, look up to the hills and know where your help comes from.

Be encouraged that he loves you with his being, so don't run away from him just because you have trouble seeing. I urge you to keep on going because in every season you'll experience his overflowing. You may ask, of what? The abundance of his spirit in which he pours out on all men/women, his Holy spirit in which will teach and guide you again and again. I understand the pain you feel but please don't give up because the enemy comes to steal and the battle is real. I just pray right now that father God would comfort you right where you are and that you would gain revelation that you'll never have never run afar.

He's with you and takes your hand yet sometimes we don't see or are able to understand. Just call on the name of Jesus with your arms opened wide; just know that you don't have to hide. He comes to save and set the captives free; yes, he came for you and even came for me.

That whisper in the quietness can move mountains and still the storm, just step into his presence into his love and warmth.

Pain (Child Birth)

Broken pieces on my floor

Quick!

I close the curtains and shut all the doors.
They'll hear or they'll see, oh I'm so scared they will
judge me.

How many times I hide myself away and cry but
when I'm around you I say "yes, yes I'm fine" such a
lie isn't it that we have adapted into the church.

We don't seek, we don't search, I lie awake all
through the night praying to GOD to comfort my heart
then I'll know I'll be alright.

I finally fall asleep hearing your voice, as deep cries
out to deep; your presence is layered thick upon my
skin, I can feel your love surrounding me like the inner
strength from deep within.

Ohh father your always with me through thick and
thin even threw the nitty gritty sin.

You love me so much father this I know because the bible tells me so. Its hard yano this pain that I feel it's like a rounda bout, some kind of ferris wheel.

It's like a raging war, a battle that seems to break out in my mind; repeating the same scenario time after time.
But I see, I see past the pain and look into your heart because you're always the same and your LOVE always remains.

I feel better already, is that because I'm letting go?
Here! Take it! Why is this process way to slow? Will I ever move on? It feels like the hold is way to strong.
Child birth isn't even this long.
Ohh daddy. I'm going back to sleep, please wake me up and tell me when it's

COMPLETE...

Deep cries out to Deep

You touch my heart; you're close and not far,
your beauties like a shooting star.
Your presence so divine and oh I can't believe I
am yours and you are mine.
This hope so real, this hope so true and this
hope I hold, I'll never lose.
To give is to receive and to receive is to believe.
Awe LORD, you are truly awesome in all of your
ways that I'm so in love
Until I meet you face to face.

"Father I will count the days. The sound my heart makes when I hear your voice and the joy my spirit feels oh that I rejoice.
The depth within me cries out for more and the hunger in my soul is eager to explore.
Fill me oh Father from head to toe fill me oh and cause me to overflow that I may know your love and see your heart."

Favouritism

Treating everyone equally in the eyes of our Lord
causes less pain in which we put down our sword.
Equality encourages and builds up, whereas
favouritism is like a volcano about to erupt.
I get that everyone has needs in which we must meet;
but favouritism only teaches people to compete.
Next time think about how you treat people in the
crowd because favouritism's actions are obvious and
loud.
Let's look at a story in the bible and see; we must
remember that
UNITY is key...
Jacob favoured Joseph and treats him oh so well, but
his brothers were so angry and threw him down a
well.
They decided amongst themselves to get rid and sell
him into slavery and there he went waving his
brothers a bid farewell. Wow!! What such evil that
grew from just one seed, favouritism kills if you can
see what I mean. Love each one the same as your
meaning to go on, everyone is different and unique
but in Christ they belong.

Adulterous woman was my name

They dragged me out of bed and into the street; I was
naked not even covered by my own bed sheet. My
hair ragged back as my body layered bare, they
chucked things at me and began to stare. I held back
every tear as I felt a dread of despair; I bowed my
head down in so much shame. I heard laughter and
felt tormented as they took away my NAME! Fear ran
up my body as I heard them say "she's an adulterous.
She needs to pay" To scared to lift my head, thinking
that I'm as good as dead. And that's when I heard
them loud and clear knowing that death was near. I
heard the sounds of rocks ringing, I heard all their
hands swinging; echoing right into the atmosphere
Then SILENCE...

There was a man named Jesus who stood up straight
and tall. He broke the silence as what he said
convicted them all. Each one left from old to young, I
was shaking to scared to run. He came so close and
asked me where my accusers had gone, "didn't even
one of them condemn you" he said, "No Lord" I said
as I slowly began to lift up my head. He then looked
deep into my eyes and said "Neither do I as you saw,
now go... go and sin no more. Then something

happened within my soul which was right at the core so deep on the inside, for the first time I felt...
ALIVE!!!!!!!!

You see
this woman, this woman was me but now I'm a child of God who has been set free. I've been given a new name, I'm no longer bound to shame; I'm free to be who my father has called me to be, free from you and free from me.

I'm free to dance and free to sing, I'm free to praise – just to worship HIM!! Jesus is his name enthroned on high, a lamb lead to the slaughter and a living sacrifice. He gives salvation, forgiveness and restoration!!

He gives it freely to a broken nation from generation to generation. Calling people out of darkness and into the light calling people to stand in his truth not by their might but by his spirit, his power so as you stand you would become a strong tower. An oak tree of his righteousness for all to see, as a display to show the world the lord's majesty and his GLORY...

Chains

Save me from this pain inside, I'm not one of those
who can easily hide. It feels like hell! Fire blazing all
threw my veins. Please someone help me unravel
these chains.
I open my mouth and let out a sound, it scared me to
death as it shook the ground.
I'm trapped between the devil and the see so I shout
please someone just come and rescue me. I look up
to the window and all I see are people staring and
just walking past me so I shake and chains
"Just listen me, I just wanna be FREE"
A few hours later I'm still all alone and I've found that
my heart is turning into stone.
I'm tired and I'm cold sat on this wet floor but I can't
help myself from looking at the door. The room goes
still as I sit and think about my life; death comes in
"Turn to the knife"
I wish I could go back and change the events time
with my family I would have spent. Death says
"you've got no more chances this is your last use it
widely ...TICK TOCK...
(Silence) NO!!
I'm no longer a slave to my PAST.

I'm no longer
A SLAVE
to my past

A Wise Tale

They say "ignorance is bliss" suppose it is when
you're the one doing it. The silence of not listening to
one another and disunity between a sister and a
brother, Satan firing at you with the same old
LIES...
LIES...

You're constantly in your head not being able to sleep
as you crawl into bed.
Eyes wide open as you count the dints in the wall,
stumbling again and again, wisdom says "be careful
because pride comes before a fall" your heart is
desperate for peace and to sort things out and you
wrestle with unforgiveness whilst in doubt.

The thoughts come "why should I apologise when
she did... that kind of attitude is dangerous, so bin
and get rid! Where called to be forgiving, loving and
understanding but I get what you mean when people
can be demanding.

Especially Christians within the church congregation, we need to be careful in how we teach the next generation. We should love and value one another and aim to wash each other's feet, that's when you know the fathers love is complete.

When we serve one another without motive or gain but we do it out of a heart that is sustained, I've learnt this tale again and again.
Freedom is lived out of a life of forgiveness and openness, just believe it and confess!
And keep speaking life over your circumstances and just let the burden go, live a life of intimacy because out of it you will overflow.
LOVE.
HIS LOVE...

In This Moment

Broken down and washed out, no more strength to
even break out! I shout out, lash out and no one
hears my cry, feeling broken deep on the inside.
HEAR ME!! Do you hear the cry of my heart?
AHHHH!!! I scream... as I fall apart. I lie on the floor in
a mess once more, with nothing! I'm weak, I have no
strength.

In that moment my cry reaches my FATHERS heart
and in an instant I know he's never far apart, that still
quiet whisper reaches its way towards my ear and
that's the voice my spirit longs to hear.
My child I'm here there's no need to fear; come now
just take my hand because I want to show you
something, something that will help you to
understand.

We go to a place that's far away! We go to a place
where I long to stay, I can feel the beat of his heart as
I curl into his Chest.

I can feel a warm presence surrounding me as I close my eyes to rest. Ohh father can I not stay here with you forever? Me and you just us two together.
No noise or chaos no grief or loss, no hurt or any pain...

All I feel is peace as I watch you bring down the rain whilst your love pours out on me again and again.
MY EYES OPEN...

You're not there. But! I hear you; I hear your sound in the open air.

I understand now father, I hear you loud and clear as your love is just pouring over me and gushing out the fear.

Thank you that you listen and care and thank you that you're always there, here and everywhere.
I LOVE YOU SO MUCH

Letting Go Of Guilt

I speak

Peace be still...

(so much chaos in my head)

Be still!

To the waves that crash against one another within my soul, be still to the voices that try to take control. Be still to those demons that rage against my mind time after time, be still to those who are eager to destroy my heart and be still to the death of my past and the words that try to voice

"I CAN'T".

Be still to the pain of regret as I grieve for the lost little girl in my dreams, the one that lost her mum...

"Where is she, have you seen? Have you seen?"

The memories of a baby smiling with joy to a dark looking feature holding her toy "She can't see; she can't see".

Not watching as she crawled with gladness, not watching as she lost her hope with sadness "I see, I see, I see".
Her eyes light up when she sees my face, I see her look back at me as I hold her in my embrace, I see now what I have done and I see where it all begun.
Ohh father I grieve, grieve and now I believe because I now see...
ALL SHE WANTS IS HER MUM...
"Good lord, what have I done? Forgive my heart for it is so far apart"
I've been so focused on getting myself right that I've neglected my daughter by refusing to fight, just letting go and walking away.
Well no more father, because today I will stand strong and begin to pray
I pray to the heavens and ask for you to open wide, right now father over her life.

Fight From Within

Torn down, where is my crown? Blindly I roam as I
search the phonebook threw my phone.

I'm alone

I'm alone

All I seem to do is gain confusion as I think, battling
inside and pushing away the drink, fighting for
freedom every single day shutting my mouth not
willing to say what is going on deep down in my soul,
gripping a hold of myself before I lose control.

I scream

I scream

This pain, it never seems to go away. Dam you!! What
more can I say? I'm so sick, so sick and tired of being
up so late practically wired. I see food so I binge until
I feel sick and crawl into my bed, EMBARRASSED
and ASHAMED as I hide the wrappers burying my
head.

I eat

I eat

It feels so good and something I find hard to defeat!!
It's like lust which feels so good at the time but in the
end it reaps a corrupt mind.
Help me father as we wrestle with sin, lust, gluttony,
gossip, jealousy, pride, malice and gambling.
Help me to find comfort from your spirit from deep
within, pour out your mercy and grace until we are
overflowing.
You're so kind father to freely forgive us of our sins
yet we walk around utterly blind, the solution is to
renew our mind.
But we want a quick fix so quick and fast, if that's the
case I'm sure it won't last. I want something that will
sustain me and hold me in place; I want to see your
transforming power fall in this place...
Jesus

__Thinking__

Carry me daddy into your safe place, let me see
you... your beauty shines upon my face. Your
presence is all that I need, I just need to continue to
declare
"I WILL SUCEED"
Lies are toxic daddy and there like a poisonous gas
that stems from just one seed, Ohh give me a hunger
for your word so I can feed. Yano daddy when I think
about your faithfulness and all that you've done I start
to ponder the work in me that you've already begun.
How I desperately want to look like Jesus; your son...
I will stand... I will, but.... what if I
RUN
No, no!

I'll stand because you're my father and you have me in the palm of your hand, you know me and understand. I've seen too much before my eyes, it's a battle not to get tangled with the enemy's lies.

but I saw you, I saw you

PART MY RED SEA

I saw you open it WIDE....

Over my circumstances and over many lives. I saw my Egypt finally disappear and you showed me that I didn't have to fear.

I had one more look at my past as I waved goodbye and I saw that old me finally die.

I saw a new person rise up as I began to take one step forward into a new place – I saw you become my Lord and I felt your embrace.

Forgiveness is a gift you give yourself

I just want us sit in this moment
Let's reflect...

Sometimes we may feel stuck between a rock and a hard place but if we don't come to that place of letting go of the pain, offences, rejection and hurt we harbour in our hearts then we will only hold ourselves captive. Someone once said to me that un-forgiveness is like drinking poison and expecting the other person to be in pain or to hurt the way you hurt. I know that the abuse I faced in my past left me feeling all kind of ways and because of this I grew to really hate myself so much that I didn't even recognise who I had become. The Lord came to me in his love and said **"Sarah, let me take your pain and let me heal your heart"** I was scared because pain was all I knew and without it I didn't have anything, **who was I?**

Jesus reached his hand out to me **"Will you let go, let go of the past?" and forgive those who hurt**

you, those who rejected you, those who abandoned and abused you?

Today I am asking you the same question that Jesus once asked me, will you choose to let go and forgive so that you can become free?

During this time, I want us to create some space to do the following

Let's pray

Father I come before you right now asking that you would help me just to be open and honest about how I really feel. Help me to have an open heart towards you, take away any fear from me right now I pray in Jesus name Amen.

1. *Get a piece of writing paper and a pen*

2. *Cut off any distractions and noises around of you*

I want you to take a deep breath and begin to wright about those who have mistreat you, caused you pain and hurt you. I want you to be honest and allow your emotions to be expressed onto the writing paper, when you feel enough is enough I want you to stop. Take another deep breath and allow the Holy Spirit to fill you with his inner peace and stillness, take your time and just be moved by his leading.

Now, I want you to continue to wright about this person but this time I want you to wright blessings over them and their lives, this will release them from your heart.

I bless them in Jesus name and release them to you Father and I let them go out of my hands out of my control.

I forgive- don't be in a rush to move on, allow yourself time and grace to be able to walk this out as it will be raw and very painful. Maybe go take a bath or spend some time relaxing, put some worship music on and just allow yourself to rest. *My prayer is that you would know his resting place and healing.*

Speak Out

SPEAK OUT IS ABOUT USING THE WORD OF GOD AND ALLOWING IT TO BREAK DOWN THE LIES OF THE ENEMY. THIS WILL SET YOU FREE AND CAUSE YOU TO SEE YOUR TRUTH WORTH IN JESUS CHRIST. BEGIN TO DECLARE THIS OVER YOUR LIFE, THERE IS POWER WITHIN THE TONGUE AND AS YOU BEGIN TO SPEAK OUT YOU WILL SEE CHAINS BREAK OVER YOUR LIFE AND OVER YOUR MIND IN JESUS NAME.

Speak Out

Your

VALUED

ACEPTED

Never REJECTED

HOLY AND BLAMLESS

Without a cause, broken was his body and spilt

was his blood over all of your flaws!

Ya see, my friend...

Your

LOVED

REDEEMED

RESTORED

And

SET FREE

For in him, you were created to be

VICTORIOUS

As Deep Cries Out I'm Yours

You whisper in my ear, the words I long to hear. You tell me to be brave, you say to persevere. You say I'm not alone and to you my heart belongs, the war is all around but I stand on solid ground and I'm yours, I'm yours.

As deep cries out to deep, as deep cries out to deep I'm yours, I'm yours. As deep cries out to deep, as deep cries out to deep I'm yours, I'm yours. As deep cries out to deep, as deep cries out to deep I'm yours, I'm yours.

You say that you understand and its time to take your hand, my spirit hears your sound I was lost but now I'm found. Lead me the way for today is the day...
I'm yours, I'm yours

As deep cries out to deep, as deep cries out to deep I'm yours, I'm yours. As deep cries out to deep, as deep cries out to deep I'm yours, I'm yours. As deep cries out to deep, as deep cries out to deep I'm yours, I'm yours.

And now I'm safe in your arms, the oceans are made calm
And I belong.
Yes, I belong.
I, belong to you.
As deep cries out to deep, as deep cries out to deep I'm yours, I'm yours. As deep cries out to deep, as deep cries out to deep I'm yours, I'm yours. As deep cries out to deep, as deep cries out to deep I'm yours, I'm yours.

Ponder

As I wait.
As I wait.

Breathing in and just receiving your grace.

Awe just being face to face delights my soul as it
yerns for you from deep within, you shadow me
from the darkness as it tries to creep in.
Standing against it with the voice from deep
inside, I am a light that no darkness or man can
hide.

My heart burns for you as I sit and wait for you to
take me home, waiting in the midst of the battle
for your promises to come.
When the sun is out by day not by night I see
your glory shinning bright, it reminds me of how
glorious you are and that no darkness or man
can distinguish your great light.

How majestic is my God, you're the creator of
the beginning and end?
Yet somehow you want to be my friend

Such love is this!

So pure so true, you ask for nothing in return...
Yet...
father as we learn
We see
We see
That the creator of this universe so majestic and
powerful in all of his ways just wants...
To be with?
Me.

The Waves

I see the waves

I see the freedom

I see the depth of your love

It extends and reigns down from heaven and is

pictured like a dove

But then I see the waves and there coming

against me but I see your mighty hand

RISING UP

And I'm gonna fight!

And I'm gonna fight, to come into your presence

I'm made to overcome in every circumstance

and when the storms are raging I'm gonna

choose to dance.

No matter how big the wave is you are greater

and you are higher than any other, holding me

like a father and closer than a brother.

Your grace! it abounds in the whirlwind of my
heart and your love gives me a knowing that
you're with me, we will never be apart.

I will FIGHT
I will FIGHT

Cause me to see, father cause me to see, above
the pain and above the wave of disappointment
Because in your presence where you hold me
close is where I feel the most content
I take a deep breath in and breathe out...
PEACE

Lazarus

Lazarus

Come out

My body felt release when I heard him shout

(It got louder)

Lazarus!

Come out

My hands and feet wrapped with strips of linen and clothe around my face, am I back in this place? Everything seems dark and I'm finding it hard to breathe and what is this on my face because I can't even see. But I can hear the beat of my heart as my mind begins to fade and stand in utter silence feeling dismayed
I heard him again

TAKE OFF THE GRAVE CLOTHES AND LET HIM GO

I slowly took off the grave clothes until they were no more.

I see things so clear as Jesus stands before my eyes...

I was DEAD. But now I have been RAISED TO LIFE

<u>Glimpse</u>

Let me hide you, take my hand and walk with me
because I want you to understand - It's time to look
up daughter...
Tell me what you see?
I see the stars?
Look again and tell me what you see?
I see....
(I'm looking intently)

I see a tree... Ermm yeah I see a really big tree
standing tall which looks tons bigger than them all,
with big and thick branches hanging down with
glimmers of gold all around.

I see fruit of different shapes, sizes and colours of all
Father....
I can hear the call.

I can hear the cries of the generation; I can feel your
heart break for a broken nation. I can see JESUS, I
see salvation.

Families having restoration. People being healed and completely set free, people being plucked out from darkness and becoming a son,

gaining there true

IDENTITY

And finally gaining the

VICTORY

Being so close to you like it was meant to be
That's going to be my life isn't it, I'm going to see you revive the hearts of many not just the tens or the twenty – but a multitude of people desperate for you.
Father help me to lead them by your spirit and not my will.
In this season I'm growing, radiant and glowing and building strength on the inside; you're teaching me how to abide. Out of my inner most being will completely overflow... until that day comes when you say the word
GO

<u>Wander</u>

Father, do you dream?
I see a beautiful oak tree next to the tranquil stream.
I see the grass all cut nicely trim; ha ha ... do you
want to go for a swim?
I feel right light in your presence; it's like an aroma
yano like a nice fragrance.
Wow! Taste and see is what you say I should believe,
Father won't you hold my hand and never ever leave.
Let's walk together and you can tell me all about the
stars.
Thank you so much father for healing my scars,
woahhhh!!! Look how bright the star's shine. I close
my eyes and hold onto this moment which is so
divine.
The sky is like a midnight wave that flows back and
forth going right through the majestic north. I close
my eyes and begin to ponder; as I think deeply,
"I'm in awe at your WANDER.

Emmanuel, God With Us

Emmanuel, God with us
Jesus died for you; you're redeemed by his blood.
Well what does that mean? Have you heard? Have
you seen? A very real story revealing Gods glory
No, he wasn't just a baby in a manger or a little kid
who fled from danger; he's not a super hero or a
power ranger. Truth is, he is God the father, Jesus the
son and Holy Spirit all crammed into one – who
created the earth and formed the stars, that's where it
all begun

You see. God created Adam then came Eve, I know
right hard to believe. They had dominion over all the
earth and was created to submit and to serve, but
then the snake came and they were fooled and dece
ived. They ate from the tree covered in shame and
covering themselves in fig tree leaves, and that's the
story of how sin came.

The world itself turned upside down, from generation
to generation wanting to wear Gods crown. Well what
could God do? He sent a prophet, a judge and a king
which obviously didn't work in which he then tried a

different avenue. Miracle after miracle, sign after sign. God sending help time after time
We see redemption; we see restoration and God crying out to a broken nation. Then 400 years of silence

NOTHING

Then Jesus came to bring salvation. Ya see my friend; the cross is not about you or about me. It's not even about the decorations you put upon your Christmas tree

HEAR ME!

Can you see? 2000 years ago Jesus died for you, yes! He died for me. He died to square the debt over your sin, he died so that you can have abundant life deep within. He dies for relationship, to restore us back to himself. By his stripes we have been healed, yes that's right we have been made well. It's not about money or about wealth. You can have everything in the world and still feel like you don't belong but Jesus loves and accepts you and gives your heart a new song. I'm not trying to convince you so don't get me wrong.

WOW! Isn't this awesome, I bet your thinking but how? Now that's where faith kicks in, believing without seeing is where your journey begins.
I'll leave you to have a think about what's been said but just remember this

GODS NOT DEAD!

He will never leave or forsake you, it doesn't matter what you say or do. Reach out and ask for forgiveness, yes! Speak your sins out that's it confess. His grace will help you so don't you worry; just remember that it's not a race so no need to hurry.
So

Let's reminisce, go on and have a think; I'll leave you with this

EMMANUEL GOD WITH US

Respond and don't dismiss

<u>As I Wait</u>

I stand there rearing to go, my hands are ready and
I'm just so desperate to receive his overflow.
My hands are waving in the air and my eyes are shut
tight as I stand there ready to worship my king.
Then I start to let out a tune and begin to sing. I begin
to strive my way through and let out a shout, the
moment comes and I start to dance and praise out.
I begin to sing in the spirit and start to pray "What
more can I do Lord? what more can I say"
He quietens my spirit and I start to just wait in his
presence, losing myself in his love once again.
In that moment I remember that his promises are "Yes
and Amen".

STILLNESS

not even a sound as I slowly open my eyes and my
face is on the ground. I'm on my knees and my heart
cries out.
Show me your glory in this season of doubt.

SILENCE BREAKS OUT

His holiness fills this place as I see each woman and
man on their face
We wait, we wait
Father speak
we are listening.

Warrior Bride

(co-author Laura Murray)

I am the jewel in his crown

No longer will I choose to bow my head down

I am now seated in heavenly places

I am bought with a price that saved me

I am lavished in his fragrance

His presence that saturates me

I am the warrior bride

I am his and he is mine

He causes my face to shine

And now, now is the time...

I will arise, I will arise

Because I am a daughter of the most high...

The Lord Is Calling Out To A Generation

He's calling out to a generation that want to see his spirit move across this nation.

He's calling out to the dreamers within the church, that don't know which way to go SO forever they search. To the Peter's that see the visions and walk in the boldness and to the women who love much because they have received forgiveness. From the Abrahams to the Sarah's that wants to walk in the promise, to those who are desperate to believe like doubting Thomas.

To the Timothy's that want to bring the truth and the fire and to the prayer warriors who fast like the Ester's and the Nehemiah's. To the Mary's that no how to rest and to the Martha's who serve, serve at their best. To the David's that bring creativity and write from a heart of affliction and to the Mary Mandolin's and the legion's that have been set free from addiction.

To the Barnabas who think "My gift of encouragement is nothing much" The Lord is calling you out to grow in confidence so that you can learn how to trust. From the power from within, HOLY SPIRIT is your teacher and that my friend is where it begins. He wants to teach you how to tune in and listen to the rhythm of the father's heart; he wants to teach you how to hold up your shield of faith to stop those fiery darts. He's calling out to a people that would stand upon his word and not just the history books and the preachers that you've heard. He wants to journey with you, by building his relationship with you on biblical truths with honour and respect like Naomi and Ruth. He wants to raise up a people with passion and devotion, none of this "It's about me" centre stage commotion. Living a life style of worship onto him; **SO WHO ARE YOU WHEN THE MUSIC FADES**, because it's not about platforms or silly parades. He wants to see his people move in purpose and destiny, discovering their **IDENTITY** and finding their **AUTHENTICITY**

He wants to raise up the next generation of revivalist and fill them up so that he can then send them out! He wants us to take a stand
TOGETHER...

OPEN YOU'RE MOUTHS AND LET OUT A SHOUT

Bringing a new sound for all to see, the father's splendor

Revealing his **GLORY**

"IT'S TIME, ARISE AND SHINE FOR YOUR LIGHT HAS COME"

Intimacy

I come to your table to share in your communion;
I spend time in your presence seeking your union.
You are beautiful in all of your ways, oh Lord I could
sit hear gazing into your eyes for hours even days.
I just feel so safe with you sat so close; you just
eliminate every negative thought and every lie and fill
me up with so much purpose.

You shift my perspective and set me free from this
slave and victim mentality, i feel like your love takes
over every time you open up to speak. You my Lord
are so full of strength, so fearless, humble and meek.
I could stay here with you forever my king

(Pause)

You cause my heart to sing.
You're the lover of my soul, you just make me whole.
I draw closer into your chest and shut my eyes, thank
you so much my lord that you spared my life. I love
you so much and cling tight to your robe.
I could stay this way forever, just you and me
together

I feel like a child in my father's arms and see you as a
mother who is nurturing and calm
I hear the sound of the stream
I breathe in peace
Lord, is this a dream?
I open my eyes and I'm layed on my face, I lift myself
up and take breathe and still feel his warm embrace.

Walking Free

I get up
I get dressed
I get ready to go
My armour intact
I'm ready for the overflow, I step into position the
fight has begun. I stand proclaiming the Lord's victory
because the battle has been won.
Fear tries to creep in and takes me out, So I raise up
the sword of the spirit and let out a shout
It's for freedom that Christ has set me free
For in him I am created to be
A child of God
Who the son sets free, Is free indeed
I'm walking free, I'm walking free
I declare
victorious! victorious!
I am victorious

She Has Risen

She was bound by chains and covered by a thick air
of darkness, pollution filling its people with toxic
illnesses, sickness and pain.
Walking through the street you can almost feel her
pain, you can see the women covered in shame and
the same religious acts performed again and again.

From the Muslim's performing their sacrifices, to the
Catholics sitting in the street and then to the atheist
who is sat next to the fountain trying to eat.

So much filled the air that it was hard to breathe,
tourist, students and missionaries coming but then
they had to leave.

We were desperate and in need of a hope to arise, to
breakdown this culture of lies...
That is when I saw it as clear as day, there was a
woman who just stood still and began to pray;
standing forward with something in her hand and
then along came her friend and other's started to
follow and together they stand.

You could see the colour change in the sky, and then we heard about this man that came to die. His presence brought love and such a peace and over the next few months his presence started to increase. There was a group of people that looked like an army at war healing the broken as they started to pray for the sick more and more.

The heaven's started to pour out and the people would begin to shout

"JESUS

forever is your name enthroned on high, holy is his name"

There was a joy restored to her and she was never the same!

A new sense of freedom started to reign

she had finally found her crown and then moved forward and put on her gown

she lifted her head up and let out a beautiful sound

She was no longer lost in darkness

She was no longer bound

FREEDOM

BE STRONG AND COURAGEOUS

ISAIAH 41 V 13

FOR I AM THE LORD YOUR GOD WHO TAKES HOLD OF YOUR RIGHT HAND AND SAYS TO YOU, DO NOT FEAR, I WILL HELP YOU.

ENDURANCE

LOVE

hope

faith

peace

courage

servanthood

strength

LIFE

My name is Sarah Clarke and one day I will help many broken people FIND FREEDOM

selfless

redeemed

JOY

BE STILL AND KNOW THAT I AM GOD

<u>Hands</u>

I want you to leave this book encouraged and stirred
on, not just to walk in victory but fulfilling your God
given destiny and purpose over your life. Here is
something I want to share with you out of my own
personal journey.
Along time ago God asked me what I wanted to do
with my hands and what kind of women did I want to
become.
My answer was a woman who helped others
sacrificially and one of great joy and strength. I
wanted to be a woman who walked in immeasurable
love and compassion for others. A woman who walks
in boldness and has unmovable faith to help and to
encourage others.
I want to ask you the same question.
What kind of woman or man do you want to
become?
How do you want God to use your hands?
I want you to take a short time to think and mull this
question over, ask the holy spirit to help you.
Ready?
Take a pen and draw around your hands or around
one hand onto a plain piece of paper. When you have

done that wright onto the paper of what comes into your heart, you can't go wrong with this.

Don't be afraid, dream big because with God nothing is impossible!!

Luke 1:37

For nothing will be impossible with God

"Believe"

God used normal people in the bible that just believed

BUT GOD

He takes broken men and women and transforms them and uses them and then sends them out to change the world. He loves us and wants us to believe that we are appointed and anointed for service. His workmanship to be used to show and to reveal Gods glory in the earth so that many will believe in him.

Ephesians 2:10 (NLT)

For we are God's masterpiece. He has created us a new in Christ Jesus so we can do the good things planned long ago.

Jeremiah 1:5 (NLT)

I knew you before I formed you in your mother's womb. Before you were born I set you apart and appointed you.

We are called

We have been chosen

We have been appointed

We are world changers

I'm encouraging you and believing with you that what you write on your hands onto the piece of paper will come to pass in the mighty name of Jesus Christ

Amen

Printed in Poland
by Amazon Fulfillment
Poland Sp. z o.o., Wrocław

63562738R00054